POLIO and ME

in
Nigeria and Malawi, Belgium, England
And Other Places, 1955 - 1998

by
KEN BARNES C.B.E.

With a Foreword by
SIR JULIAN CRITCHLEY

Published by K. Barnes
29 Bearwater
Charnham Street
Hungerford
Berks., RG17 0NN

© 1998, K. Barnes

ISBN 0 9534567 0 6

Printed in Great Britain by Fieldfare Publications, Cambridge.

Dedicated to

Lesley

We met in October 1950
We married in June 1953
Our children are:
Caroline born in England in May, 1955;
Nicholas born in Nigeria in May, 1958; and
Julian born in Malawi in January, 1961
Lesley died on 12 April, 1976.
My life was in her care while living;
Her memory lives on ever strong in my heart.

CONTENTS

Foreword by Sir Julian Critchley   vii

Paralysis and Convalescence   1

Living with Disabilities   17

Retirement   45

Plates

Between pages iv-v
1 Frontispiece Author in wheelchair with George Jaffu (his successor in Malawi) and Fiona Jaffu, Gray's Inn, London, July, 1998.
Between pages 44-45
2 Author, 1954
3 Early Steps, 1955
4 With daughter, Caroline, Enugu, 1957
5 Abak swimming-pool, 1959
6 Nung Ibesit Leper Village, 1959
7 With Caroline and Nicholas, the Acropolis at Athens, 1965
8 SUCOMA sugar-mill, Malawi. 1968
9 World Bank meeting, Washington, 1968

Author in wheelchair with George Jaffu (my successor in Malawi) and his daughter Fiona, on the occasion of the latter's being called to the Bar, Gray's Inn, London, July 1998.

FOREWORD
by Sir Julian Critchley

Some years ago in the Royal Shrewsbury Hospital I was obliged to give my medical history to a young male hospital nurse. I told him that in 1949, at the age of 18, I fell ill with Polio. "What's that?" he asked. "Infantile Paralysis" I replied. "Never heard of it" was his reply.

I made no complaint. Thank God for Messrs Salk and Sabin. Sadly they came on the scene too late for me as they did for the author of this book who tells an all too familiar story of courage and determination when he, too, was struck down by the virus in Africa in 1955.

I was comparatively lucky. I woke on the fourth day of my sickness to find that my right leg was weak. I could not stand on my toes. The paralysis, for which my parents had anxiously waited since I had become sick on Guy Fawkes' Day, had afflicted my leg as far as the buttock. The irony was that my father was a neurologist, and, as such, a specialist in the disease. As Dean of the National Hospital, Queen Square, he found a bed for me in Annie Zunz, where I spent six weeks recuperating. I was treated by a formidable Scots physio called Miss Hurn who stretched and strengthened what was left of my leg muscles with exercise and an electric machine.

The end result was that I could walk with a barely perceptible limp, but I could not run. I learnt to wait for buses, although my parents promptly brought me a bike on which to exercise.

As a result of polio I escaped National Service and Korea and went to the Sorbonne in Paris instead. It was an ill wind!

Mr. Barnes writes towards the end of his brave account of his life of the Late Effects of Polio (LEP). My reprieve lasted forty years or so until1992, when the disc controlling my withered leg bust ("extruded" is the term) spreading the paralysis so that I am now registered disabled. I can barely walk with the aid of a crutch and cannot stand or sit in comfort. In consequence, I was obliged to give up my seat in Parliament.

Was this catastrophe the consequence of a latent virus or of a spinal injury caused by my limp? Nobody seems to know. What I do know is that there are many of us who now face, after the lapse of time, the silent return of a terrible disease. Yet I was luckier than many; more fortunate certainly than Ken Barnes. I certainly think that nearly everything in my lifetime has improved, save possibly for pop music. But all praise is due to Salk and Sabin who saved my children and grandchildren from the terrors of Polio.

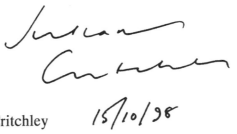

\Julian Critchley   15/10/98

PARALYSIS AND CONVALESCENCE
1955-1956

One Sunday morning at the beginning of March 1955, I walked the few hundred yards from my house to The Residency at Calabar where I had an office. I was 24 years old, married for 20 months (with my wife expecting our first child in three months time) and a Cadet in the Colonial Administrative Service, serving in Eastern Nigeria.

I was moving to a new job the next morning and wished to ensure that all the papers and files that I had been dealing with were left in good order for my successor. I worked steadily for a couple of hours but was conscious of an increasingly severe headache and a general feeling of malaise leading to an inability to concentrate on what I was doing (it was discovered later that I had burnt the most recent copy of the Top Secret Colonial Local Cipher instead of the older version which it had replaced! I never knew this Cipher to be used so the practical consequences were not great but my destruction of the Calabar copy meant that all other copies throughout the Empire were 'compromised'!). So, about mid-day I walked home in the fierce sun (the normal temperature in Calabar was around 90°F - 35°C - and humidity a steady 85%) intending to return in the afternoon to finish what I had to do.

After lunch, I lay down hoping that a rest would cure my headache. It didn't. I developed a fever instead.

1

The next morning my wife sent a message over to the office saying that I was ill: which was thought inconvenient. That evening, the senior Medical Officer on the station, a surgeon, came to call. By this time all my joints were aching, my temperature was rising, then falling sharply for a time, then rising again, each time slightly higher. The doctor didn't know what it was but prescribed, I think, aspirin and the current anti-malarial drug.

That night I could not sleep or indeed stay still for the pain in my joints.

The next day was a repetition of the previous one. The Medical Officer called again at my wife's request but made it clear that he thought that I just had a fever and was exaggerating things - although my wife and I were certain that it was not malaria.

That night a tropical storm broke with lightening, thunder and a sudden gale. I climbed onto the windowsills in our bedroom to close the thick wooden shutters (the windows had no glass) to keep out the driven rain. When I had nearly finished a leg gave way and I fell to the floor. After a few minutes though it recovered its strength and I was able to crawl into bed. I think that I hallucinated most of that night.

Next morning when I went to the lavatory my legs went from under me and I fell to the floor. My wife called the servants who lifted me into bed and then sent an urgent message for me to be seen again. The Medical Officer arrived and ordered an ambulance to take me to the little Cottage Hospital before going on to his other duties. There was no ambulance however so my wife sent for two of my colleagues who carried me out to their saloon car, to the hospital and then, with an arm around each of their shoulders, up the wooden steps.

I don't remember much of the next week. The paralysis grew worse, my breathing was affected, the doctors (three of them by now) appeared to have no idea of what was wrong (although the nurses did: but, as they told my wife, "It wasn't for us to tell the doctors").

At some point it was decided that I had polio and that I should be flown to Lagos 600 miles away accompanied by my wife. She had 24 hours to pack up all our belongings, hand-over our cat to a friend and pay-off our servants. The plane was a DC-3, not pressurised of course, and some seats were taken out so that I could lie on my stretcher; a catheter was inserted to take care of urination during the 5 hour flight (it was just the normal commercial flight, calling at one or two other towns on the way).

In Lagos an ambulance took me to the Creek Hospital; my wife was billeted upon a married couple whom we did not know but who had a spare room. But what then?

At the Creek Hospital I was in an isolation ward, where the word 'isolation' meant just that for most of each day. I rarely saw an English doctor or nurse and although the Nigerian nursing orderlies were helpful they had had little or no training in how to deal with polio patients. Since I knew nothing about the disease itself this could have had serious consequences for me (indeed, may have done so). On one of my first days there, for example, wishing to go to the toilet (and wishing also to prove to myself that I was on the way back to normality), I asked an orderly to help me out of bed and then to support me in shuffling across the ward to the WC As it happened a doctor came in almost as we had started and ordered me straight back to bed, telling me that my only hope of recovering the use of my muscles was to lie absolutely still. I did not know; no one had told me.

Henceforward, obediently, I lay still on my back upon the bed, covered only with a sheet or towel over my loins while the sweat gathered on my chest and ran to the sheet beneath me (there was no air-conditioning in those days).

An orderly fed me; an orderly, summoned by an electric-bell attended to my toilet needs. On one occasion, at least, however, when lifted on to a bedpan, the bell was left out of reach of my left, and unparalysed, hand. I could not ring the bell, I tried calling out for help but no one came. I had to lie there as I was on the pan until, some time later, someone came in to my room on some quite unrelated matter.

My emotional day revolved around Lesley`s visits. She, however, depended for transport on when her hostess had the use of her husband's car and this did not necessarily coincide with hospital visiting hours. In my solitary ward, her visit could not possibly cause any disturbance to anyone else but the Matron (an unsympathetic dragon) did not agree. The regulations had to be enforced. Lesley paid no attention and came when she could regardless. On one occasion, however, the Matron saw her as she was leaving and chased after her, shouting. Lesley ran to the car park where her hostess was waiting and, even though more than six months pregnant, was the faster of the two!

Our problem was that we knew no one in Lagos. My wife's hosts were very sympathetic and helpful but the room had been provided on the understanding that it was only for a stay of a few nights; it was going to take much longer than that before I was anywhere near 'recovered'. So what could we do?

We could not afford a hotel room for her (indeed there were very few hotels in Lagos at that time) and there was no empty Government housing. There was nothing for us in Eastern Nigeria from which we had just come. The expected birth-date of our child was getting ever nearer and within a few days her pregnancy would be too advanced for her to fly to the UK (or anywhere else). Above all was the fact that the Federal Government in Lagos and the Government of Eastern Nigeria were two entirely separate bodies: there was no one in Lagos who had any definite responsibility for us.

We were in the depths of despair; I remember one afternoon we passed both weeping uncontrollably. It must have been after this that Lesley determined that there was nothing for it but to appeal direct to the Governor-General. She had to get through the usual barriers of officialdom and protocol designed to protect him, but eventually succeeded. Thereafter things happened at lightening speed. A Medical Board was convened on me and directed to report that I should be flown to England without delay; with rather ill grace they did as they were told. The government then booked six seats in the rear of the first-class cabin of the next available plane, three for me (or rather my stretcher), one for my wife and one each for a doctor and a nursing-sister who were to accompany me. Within three days of my wife speaking to His Excellency we were on the propeller-driven Argonaut bound for London.

Stage One of my recovery was accomplished - thanks to my wife.

My parents and my brother were at London airport to meet us and were naturally very distressed at seeing my helpless condition. There was not time, however, for the exchange of more than a few words as I was whisked off almost immediately in an ambulance to the Royal National Orthopaedic Hospital at Stanmore. They followed, saw me into my ward, exchanged a few words with the Sister and then returned, taking Lesley, to their house at Sutton Coldfield about a hundred miles away.

It was a tremendous relief to be back in England. Our problems, however, were not over. Lesley wanted to live within visiting distance of me and lodgings were not easy to find, nor did we have money to spare. She also had to arrange for a hospital maternity bed to be booked (not easy - she was told by unsympathetic hospital staff that she should have done this months before!).

By comparison, at Stanmore I had no immediate problems. There were some twenty badly paralysed men in my ward, about half of them polio victims, but the atmosphere was one of cheerfulness, almost of jollity on occasions. It was as if Fate had tried to do its worst but now we laughed - at least outwardly - in it's face. In this no doubt we were much helped by the youthful optimism of the young probationer-nurses who staffed the ward. They flirted light-heartedly with their charges and were always kind and cheerful.

The company of my fellows and hearing what they had to say about polio helped end the feeling of awful isolation that had beset me in Lagos. I was still confined to my bed but every day a physiotherapist came to exercise my limbs. On one fine sunny April day, I remember, the ward-sister arranged for the beds of those who wished to be wheeled-out onto a veranda where we could lie in the sunshine.

However, in those early days I experienced also the acute pains caused by the death of muscles in my affected limbs: but this passed.

It was at about this time that I read of the discovery by Dr. Sabin of a vaccine against polio. Inevitably all of us already paralysed were attacked by the thought, "If only it had been discovered a bit earlier...", but such thoughts got one nowhere; we just had to make do with what we had. We all hoped, nevertheless, that some new discovery might enable the eaten motor nerves to be replaced. That, perhaps, is still to come.

I was told by Professor Seddon (in whose unit I was) that, basically, my left leg and right arm were likely to be permanently paralysed, that my left deltoid and one of my right quadriceps were also out for good and that my lung capacity would be very seriously diminished. On the other hand, I was assured that I would be able to walk again (but just how well could not be said). Some discussion took place about possible muscle transplants but in the end it was decided that nothing should be done. A transplanted muscle never worked to full normal capacity and so, given my a-symmetrical paralysis, any operation might leave me worse off than before.

To encourage me in the face of this prognosis, my brother wrote to me using his left-hand to demonstrate that if he could do it, I also could learn to do so.

My first great moment came when I was allowed to sit up, get out of bed and be seated in a wheelchair. I no longer depended upon someone else to wipe my bottom! After that, once, sometimes twice, in each day I was wheeled down to the Physiotherapy block for exercises. There was a small pool there also where we could float, even swim a few strokes.

One day in late May I was dressed, put into a wheel chair and then into an ambulance with no idea where I was going. On arrival, though, I was briskly wheeled through the wards of another hospital and up to a bed where my wife lay, looking happy but tired. With her was our daughter, less than a day old.

I had always possessed a competitive nature and now I had another reason to beat the disease that had struck me and, through me, all our plans for future happiness and success. From then on, single-mindedly, I threw all my energies into exercising with a view to recovery. I wanted my physiotherapist to spend every minute getting me stronger and grudged every second she devoted to her other patients. I was measured and fitted for a calliper and began learning once more how to walk, first between bars, then unaided in the gymnasium and then - with considerable inward fear - in the open air, first on a path and then on grass.

The extra mobility that came from learning to walk, however haltingly, was an enormous booster to my morale and I began to realise that, by comparison with most other patients, I had escaped lightly. For example one, Elizabeth Twistington-Higgins, had been a ballet dancer; now she was almost totally paralysed and spent much of her time in an iron lung. Understandably she was often moody from sheer frustration so, having spoken to Lesley, I asked her if she would be a godmother to our daughter. Elizabeth agreed. She was to show her courage and perseverance against all odds throughout the next 35 years: an example few able-bodied people could equal.

Meanwhile, I was naturally becoming concerned about my future. I was on sick leave on full pay until October. I would then have six months on half-pay. Then out.

One day in early July my surgeon, Sir Herbert Seddon, said that I could go to my parent's home for a weekend. I think a nurse took me up to London and put me on a train but otherwise I have no recollection of the details of the journey and how I did it I don't know. Life in the cushioned environment of the hospital was so much easier than going out into an environment designed only for the fully able-bodied. But to be with my wife again and to see my daughter was worth the hassle a hundred times over.

On this first visit I experienced a problem going up the stairs to our bedroom; there was no rail on the left side. My father arranged for a simple wooden rail to be put up for use on future occasions and I was to experience in future no difficulty there. However, I was to find the same problem many, many times in the future in other houses (going down stairs did not present the same difficulty; I could go down backwards or forwards depending on which side the rail was situated).

I felt much happier in that I could see the progress I was making

On the next occasion that he made his rounds, Professor Seddon asked how I had got on and appeared satisfied with what I told him. He left the ward and very shortly after the Ward Sister called me in and told me that I was being discharged the next day to my parent's home. I could hardly believe the news. It was only just over three months since I had entered Stanmore on a stretcher and six months to a year's stay was usually the minimum length. I phoned my wife immediately to tell of the magnificent news and the next day, after emotional farewells to my physio and to the nurses who had looked after me so well, I left.

Stage Two of my recovery was accomplished.

There was still a long way to go. I had to learn how to do all the small but practical things - doing up buttons with my left hand, tying a tie and shoelaces with only one hand. I had learned to walk. I had to learn to walk further and faster. This was not helped by mishaps to my calliper, which was made of duralumin (a lightweight metal that had not been much used before so that I was by way of being a guinea pig). One day, shopping in Birmingham with my wife, daughter and brother, a strut suddenly buckled. I can't remember whether I fell but certainly I could no longer walk. My brother drove us to Birmingham Orthopaedic Hospital where, naively, I imagined I could obtain help, only to be told that since I was not their patient but was from Stanmore they could do nothing for me! So much for a National Health Service!

Rebuffed there, we tried a local blacksmith but his efforts, although at first sight they looked OK, were to no avail. As soon as any weight was put on the calliper it gave way. So my father lent his car to my brother to drive me down to Stanmore where a new strut was provided.

Although daily I was getting stronger my future was still completely unclear. I had had no wish since my 'teens except to be a member of the Colonial Administrative Service, to be anything other than a District Officer. Why, you may ask? It was more than just happy memories of childhood in Malaya where my father had worked for Dunlop Malayan Estates. It was not, I hope, just dreams of prestige or lust for power. Rather, I think, I am almost sure, that the wish was born from reading those lines in the Aenead where Vigil wrote that the Roman's task was the highest of all, 'parcere subjectis et debellare superbos' (spare the lowly and put down the overmighty). Certainly, the history of the British Empire shows that there were many in its service who had felt the same.

That history had shown also though that the British Government had never indulged in any particular sense of loyalty to its servants, particularly towards those who had served it overseas. So I had to contemplate the very real likelihood of being put penniless on the beach. I wrote to the Home Civil Service to ask if I could transfer to it from the Colonial Service if I could not continue in the latter. I was told that this was impossible: I would have to sit their normal entry exam the following year and take my chance against the brightest of newly graduated aspirants. It was an answer that confirmed my worries. When my father observed that he was sure that they would do something, my reply (as he ruefully observed in a letter to his own brother) was 'to bite his head off'. He, who had given up much for his children and who had spent over three and a half years interned by the Japanese, deserved better from me: but I was sick with worry.

So I continued my badgering of the Colonial Office. After what seemed an age but was actually only a week or two. I was required to report to their Consultant Physician, Dr. (later Sir) Brunel Hawes, so that he could assess my fitness.

I went into his consulting-room in a state of nervous tension, ready to suspect anyone as unsympathetic who did not do exactly what I wanted. In fact, events were to show that under his detached clinical manner he wished to do all he could to help. He could not in all honesty pass me as fit but he did not wish to rule out the eventuality that I might become so. Accordingly he gave it as his view that it was essential that I be admitted to King Edward V11's Convalescent Home for Officers at Osborne House in the

Isle of Wight for a prolonged period of full-time physiotherapy and exercise. Then he would see me again and only then - and depending on my progress - might I be passed fit for duty: or not.

It was at least a stay of sentence and for that I should have been grateful but my first thoughts were than it meant that Lesley and I would again be parted. However, there was no choice.

While we packed my clothes and made ready for me to leave my parent's house for Osborne there came a piece of good news. A friend of her father's lived in Cowes, only a few miles from Osborne, and it was arranged that she and Caroline could stay with them as paying guests for 3 weeks (at that time the wife of a resident patient at Osborne was allowed to enter the grounds only in the afternoons - nowadays they can even sleep in the same room!).

Stage Three was over; the results, though, were only half-satisfactory.

I was to remain at Osborne for 15 weeks. After three, Lesley returned to live with my parents. I wrote to her three or four times a week but I could only afford to visit her for a weekend about once a month. Money was tight and I had to meet the cost of being accommodated at Osborne (subsidised though it was) so she obtained a part-time job as a supply teacher while my mother looked after Caroline.

The care at Osborne was superb. The nurse/patient ratio was sometimes as low as 1:2 and the nurses themselves were all young and specially selected. There was a very kind occupational therapist who helped increase the dexterity of my left hand (gros-point tapestry amongst other things). Perhaps, though, the person who helped me most was a retired Army gym-instructor who had the imagination to teach me two things. One was to be able to pick myself up unaided if I fell over (which I did and do fairly often). There were always occasions when conditions were such that I couldn't do this but at the time I became able to do so on about 75% of my tumbles. The second trick he taught me was to hold my left thigh so that my weight could be transmitted to the surface in a direct vertical. This enabled me to walk short distances - around my bedroom or in the bathroom for instance - without my calliper. When doing this, I was, of course, very liable to let the leg bones stray from the exact verticality essential; then I fell. Usually, however, my falls - even on staircases - did no particular damage but many years later (in 1981) I splintered the end of my left femur and never afterwards had the confidence to repeat the trick.

Every spare minute I used to increase my stamina. The walk down to the sea was of a distance of just over a mile each way, a gentle slope down and then a similar slope back up. I did this regularly (falling over in some undergrowth on one occasion and being unable to regain my feet. I had to wait until I heard voices and then call out for assistance!). Eventually I managed to extend the distance I could walk to about five miles.

Every month I visited the Colonial Office. Every month a rather embarrassed young civil servant (usually a woman) told me that they had nothing to say to me. In November I went on half-pay.

In mid-December I was told to see the Consultant Physician again. This time Sir Brunel Hawes had good news for me. I could leave Osborne after Christmas and he would pass me fit to return to duty immediately thereafter. It was one of the more emotional moments of my life.

There were a hundred and one things to do. New tropical clothes had to be bought for my wife, our baby daughter and myself. I had to have a plastic bucket-top for my calliper (the normal leather one would have rotted with sweat in a month): the orthotist at Stanmore understood the problem immediately and one was made. My car (stored in Calabar along with our loads) had a 'manual' gear-change as was usual in those days on all but the largest cars. I could no longer use this and mobility was essential (I could not rely on my wife to drive me everywhere). I learned of a firm called Feeny & Johnson which specialised in adaptations, visited them at Brooklands, test drove a car fitted with a pistol-grip clutch mounted on the gear-lever (it worked off the exhaust manifold, whatever that may be), found it satisfactory (and was gratified to be told by their instructor that he felt perfectly safe when being driven by me!) and ordered one to be made and sent out to Nigeria.

The Queen was due to visit Nigeria and all plane flights were fully booked. The earliest date on which seats were available was the beginning of February (but I was now back on full pay - £830 p.a. including expatriation allowance! - and that was comforting).

On 3rd February 1956 my parents drove us down to Heathrow. Stage Four was over. I was rejoining the Service.

LIVING AND WORKING
WITH DISABILITIES
1956-1987

Eastern Nigeria, 1956-60

It is impossible for me to describe what kind of figure I must have presented to my future colleagues. I was slightly below normal height, sturdily built (although I appeared a good deal plumper as the need to balance required me to thrust my pelvis forward and my upper torso backwards!). Seated I probably looked normal enough. Immediately I came to stand up, however, the need for me to stoop while rising, to lock with a slight 'clicking' noise my calliper at the knee, would have marked me as 'disabled'. When I walked, the rigidity of my left leg, the lurching of my gait, the right arm hanging down motionless, all these would have proclaimed that I was what many termed, in those 'pre-politically-correct' days, a cripple. The white shorts and short-sleeved shirts that were the customary dress in Nigeria also displayed the metal bars and the leather knee-piece on my right leg and the wasted muscles of my right arm. The loss of two-thirds of my lung capacity meant that I could speak only in short bursts but how noticeable this was at the time I don't know; it is certainly apparent now. There had never been an Administrative Officer like it and I expect my future colleagues wondered what on earth they were expected to do with me.

Nigeria was experiencing a period of unforeseen but very rapid political change, which was to result in full independence in less than five years time. The role of Government was changing, its scope expanding. There were many more functions it was being expected to undertake but at the same time it was becoming increasingly difficult (because political change meant career uncertainty) to recruit from the United Kingdom. Nor, as yet, were there enough qualified Nigerians. In these circumstances there was no difficulty at all in finding an office job for me; a place could have been found for anyone who could read and write, disability or no.

So, for the next 21 months I worked in the Eastern Region government offices in Enugu, the capital of that Region. In kind it was no different to the type of Civil Service job performed by any young graduate anywhere: except that one had a great deal more responsibility and was paid rather less well than any comparably qualified Home Civil Servant. Living conditions were infinitely more comfortable than in the 'bush' where I had worked before contracting polio: there was electricity and running water even if the supplies of both were often interrupted.

There were also snakes. As a child in Malaya I'd been brought up be wary of these but there seemed to be many more in Nigeria. Adders - whether 'Puff', 'Gabon' or just `Brown' - were sleepy, torpid things until disturbed; their bite was deadly. Equally poisonous were small little snakes similar to the Indian krait. One of these once wriggled up the discharge pipe to the hand basin in my daughter's bedroom and was found there one morning by her African nanny. She screamed and the cook, who ran in, promptly brought a bucket of water simmering on the stove. The water poured over the snake killed it immediately without damaging the porcelain! I, of course, could never move swiftly enough to tackle a snake but the Nigerians were very happy to do so, using long sticks or cutlasses. Cats, incidentally, are almost as expert at killing snakes as is a mongoose and we always kept one as a pet in Nigeria.

The Feeny & Johnson adaptation for my car arrived and was fitted by a very competent young English mechanic. It was the first of it's kind ever seen in Nigeria and attracted much comment. Theoretically, I suppose, I could have driven it straight away relying on my old UK licence but I thought it best to arrange a driving test on the adapted car. The Police Superintendent made no difficulties in passing me[1].

Looking back, more than forty years on, I can see that I should have been very grateful for what I'd got. I was employed and paid. I was able to demonstrate that I could work long hours, that the quality of my work was good, that I was more than earning my salary. However, it was not the bush work that I had originally dreamed of doing, the administration of a District, 'the finest job in the world'.

Towards the end of 1957 we returned to England on leave. It was a cold winter I remember and my parent 's house was not well heated. The poor circulation in my left leg meant that it was often dawn before it had 'thawed-out' from the previous day! My progress was reviewed by Professor Seddon and he advised an arthridesis on my right wrist

---

1. I continued to use this Feeny and Hohnson aid until I left Nigeria when I sold my car; this piece of 'juju' was a decided asset in getting a good price for it.

which, due to the erratic muscular paralysis, was in danger of being pulled back to the fore-arm. This was done (the surgeon forgot to ask what angle I wanted the wrist to be fixed at; at the last moment he came hastening out of the operating theatre to ask me, already drugged from the pre-med!) and the grip of my right hand was much increased.

We were glad to return to Nigeria's warmth in early 1958 even though the East had been badly disturbed by riots, not against Britain but against various actions taken by their own recently elected Government. Many of my colleagues, especially the older ones, had decided already to take early retirement; the increasingly uncompetitive salaries (which were emphasised by the much better living conditions of those in the private sector) and their uncertain future in an independent country outweighed the interest and responsibility of the job.

I was beginning to feel the same. Life in the regional capital was expensive (and I had extra costs, e.g. clothing and shoe leather, because of my disabilities). Our second child had been born. My work was becoming increasingly responsible but there was no chance, it seemed, of earning more. The only way out that I could see was to get a posting to one of the 'bush' Divisions in Calabar Province.

My request for this met with a discouraging response. "Look, Ken", I was told, "all of us in bush from time to time have found ourselves in a riot. If necessary, we can run. You couldn't." It was quite true, but I wasn't prepared to accept it. Either I got my posting or I left: any of my blood lost in a riot would be on my own head.

As it happened, at that moment the political situation in Calabar Province required all Divisions to be headed by British officers. But the barrel was empty except for me and so, reluctantly, my request was allowed. I was posted to Abak Division as District Officer.

The Division was small - about 450 square miles in extent - but with a population of around 250,000 was densely populated. It lay in the heart of the oil-palm tree belt, trees so dense that in most places a glimpse of open sky was unusual. The land was low-lying and flat. The rainfall was about 120" a year, the temperature a steady 85° - 90°F; the humidity was around 90%. There was no tarred road into the Division but a telephone (which functioned intermittently) connected it to the outside world. There was no running water or electricity on the Government station. There were no other senior Government officers in the Division. The people were Annangs, a sub-tribe speaking a dialect of their own, suspicious of all outsiders, quick to quarrel, their razor-sharp machetes an extension of their hands which would chop a man or woman with little more thought than given to cutting palm-fruit or a path through the bush.

I was 28 with only six months 'bush' experience. I was disabled. I was also the only representative of Government in the Division, responsible for law and order, for tax collection, for the administration of justice in the 19 Courts (the Annangs were litigious as well as physically quarrelsome), the prison, Health, Education, Local Government, Public Works and hundred things beside. Yet, when I drove out of the dark, claustrophobic, all-enveloping bush and saw, clear before me, the Union Flag flying in front of my future home on a small hill ahead, my main feeling was that of pride. I had been entrusted with the responsibility for this Division and I was determined that I would show myself worthy of that trust.

I served in Abak for a year. I made any number of mistakes; that was inevitable given my lack of experience. I upset one of the local politicians to the extent that my future career could have been ruined. This man made up a cleverly crafted pack of allegations against me with the aim of trying to achieve this (including one to the effect that my disabilities prevented me from doing my job properly - which hurt) and an enquiry was held into my conduct. Fortunately, however, circumstances totally discredited him. Nevertheless, I learned to be more cautious.

I increased the revenue from tax collection; I kept pace (more or less) with the number of 'Native Law and Custom' cases that were referred to me. I kept the peace - again, more or less.

A violent criminal gang was operating in the area and one evening I learned that an itinerant trader had been attacked, half-murdered and his goods stolen almost within sight of my house. My wife and the local dispenser patched him up, gave him a sedative against shock, commandeered a lorry and had him driven to the nearest hospital while I turned out my 25 policemen and patrolled the area. It was hopeless to expect to find the gang, of course. Night had fallen and the bush was thick. But it was important to make an immediate response, which I then followed up by alerting all the local villages. In the following weeks these set up their own local groups to check the roads while I drove from one to the other to over-see their actions. We never caught anyone but the gang, 'Ama uke' (literally, `you like which?' - meaning your money or your life), ceased operating in my Division.

Some months later the injured man came to my office. One arm was permanently maimed but at least he lived; I was very touched that he had come to thank me.

My wife and I spent the New Year holiday with some friends in a nearby Division about 75 miles away and when we returned I was surprised to see a number of lorries carrying a large number of armed police under the command of a British Superintendent. I learned that during my absence a long-running dispute between two villages over land-ownership had erupted into violence. A church and a school had been burned-down but I don't think anyone had been killed although a number had sustained more or less serious wounds.

I set off in my car for the offending village, accompanied by a police orderly and an interpreter, with the police lorries following. Somehow or another, though, they got lost and when I arrived at the village I was alone with my two men. It was an awkward situation but there was nothing for it but to brazen it out. At first the village appeared deserted but I called for a chair to be brought into the clearing which served as a 'town-square'. Then seated, I summoned the elders, told them of my anger at what had been done and, after an hour or so, got them to produce about a dozen young men who were skulking in the trees and who were alleged to have led the raid. I don't know what I would have done with them, but, before my predicament became obvious, the lost police arrived clearly spoiling for a fight. They were, in fact, both shame-faced and disappointed that they had arrived too late, that their work had been done for them and that they had nothing to do but escort the hangdog group of young men to my prison! I was just relieved that there had been no more violence.

On another occasion, I found a group of very angry young men protesting about something or another, I have forgotten what. They were shouting and gesticulating (and, of course, all carried machetes). I could not get them to shut up and so I reversed my walking stick and put the crook of it round the neck of the man who was shouting loudest. His colleagues, after a moment's silence, thought this supremely funny and collapsed to the ground in loud laughter. As for the man I had snared, well, at first he was astonished and then, when he saw his colleagues laughing, he turned sheepish. The trouble was over.

One day in the dark I tripped on a storm-drain that I hadn't seen and fell. The next day my left foot (belonging to my callipered leg) was swollen so that I could not put a shoe on it, and so could not wear my calliper. A Lady Missionary Doctor in the next Division diagnosed some broken small bones in the foot and put a plaster-of-Paris cast on it, with instructions that it should stay on for at least a fortnight.

Clearly, though, I couldn't sit around for that length of time: work had to be done. I had bamboo poles cut and lashed to a strong wooden armchair. Then I arranged for four sturdy prisoners to be detailed to carry me from my house to the office and around the station. I should perhaps explain that, while prisoners were locked-up at night, during the day they did all sorts of odd-jobs, cutting grass, collecting firewood, carrying buckets of water from the nearest stream for the station's water supply, gardening, indeed almost anything. They had the minimum of supervision while doing these - I can remember the sight of a warder snoozing in the shade of a tree with his ancient rifle propped up against it, while a gang of prisoners cut the grass with machetes, singing rhythmically as they stooped to slash. So carrying me around was reasonably normal.

There were, of course, court cases to hear in one or other of the Customary Courts located throughout the Division. These could not be put off so I arranged that the Court Clerk in whatever court I was visiting should prepare similar carrying-chairs. I would then be carried from my car to my seat on a dais at one end of the building, from which, behind a rickety wooden table, I would try to find out the truth behind the tortuous cases that were put up for my judgement.

All that part of Nigeria was extremely humid. If one sat down, one left a dark, damp outline on the cushions; in bed one could see the sweat running off ones naked chest. Everyone smelt a bit and it was fortunate that the plastic bucket-top of my calliper was washable - otherwise I would have stunk like a galley slave. Washing water was head-loaded up by prisoners from the nearest stream, was polluted and even looked filthy, but in spite of that a bucket of water heated over a wood fire and poured into a tin bath was a relaxing sun-down ritual. One felt cleaner.

Drinking water - also from the local stream - had to be filtered to remove the mud and other visible impurities and then properly boiled. Brushing one's teeth was also done with this so-called sterile water; salads were meant to be washed in it as well.

Abak had a reputation for being an unhealthy station and it lived up to it as far as my family was concerned. Our young daughter and my wife caught quite bad fevers and I contracted jaundice (my wife - concerned about my conditioned - telephoned the nearest doctor and the diagnosis was by telephone!) and had to be hospitalised for three weeks. During this period the Division was in the even-more-inexperienced hands of my Nigerian Assistant (an extremely nice young man, straight out of University; he was killed in a riot a few years later). Then my son caught amoebic dysentery and nearly died (the Lady Doctor I have mentioned above put him on a saline-drip to prevent him drying-out and filled him with every known anti-biotic. It was still a pretty near thing, though).

I had spent a year in Abak and felt that I had made my point, that though disabled, I could do the job. So, when I was told that both the Governor and the Nigerian Head of the Eastern Region Civil Service wanted me up in Enugu, I didn't protest. My successor was to be a Nigerian, an Ibo, which didn't please my people very much although I explained that there would be no more white D.Os: the country was in the final stage before independence. I introduced Mr. Emeghara[2] around, took him through my very-full 'handing-over' notes, showed him the secret files, checked the cash-balances in the Treasury and gave him the key to the safe.

2. I have learned recently with much pleasure that Mr. Emeghara survived the Biafran War and had a successful career in the Nigerian Service.

An unforgettable chapter in my life was over.

It was an office job again in Enugu but I had 'acting'-rank and a substantial increase in salary. Lesley took the children to England (where my parents thought that my son Nicholas looked like a child out of a concentration camp, he was so skinny). I stayed on in Enugu for four months. It was an interesting job that involved me in inter-governmental negotiations with my (much older) counter-parts in the other Regions and brought me into contact with a number of African Ministers (including the Federal Prime Minister, later to be murdered in a coup).

I was over-due for leave in the U.K. and, although I was pressed to stay on in Eastern Nigeria, I had asked to be transferred after my leave to Nyasaland (which had a much better climate). This, a transfer on health grounds in respect both of my son and of myself, was a reason, which my Nigerian friends accepted with immediate understanding. So, after a round of farewell parties, in December 1959, I left Enugu where I had arrived with high hopes for my future career just five and half years before. Now I was departing the poorer by an arm and a leg - but what was left had been matured by experience.

Nyasaland/Malawi, 1960-71

Nyasaland, or Malawi as it was to be renamed when it became independent in 1964, is a long narrow country bordering a long narrow Lake, forming part of the Great African Rift which extended as far north as the Red Sea. The surface of the Lake was about 1500' above sea-level. It contained a number of large, high plateaux, the Vipya and the Nyika in the northern half of the country, the Shire Highlands and the Zomba and Mlanje plateaux in the South. These uplands had encouraged 'white' settlement (mostly British). These settlers, while never anywhere near as numerous as those in Kenya or Rhodesia, exerted very considerable local political influence and had been vociferously in favour of the creation of the Federation of Rhodesia and Nyasaland in 1953. The African peoples of Nyasaland, however, were always vehemently opposed to this body; they feared that Federation was no more than an attempt by white dominated Rhodesia to extend its political power to Nyasaland. They feared for their land.

There had been riots in 1953 when the British Government had created the Federation. These had been put down with minimum force but the opposition had remained. In 1958 Dr. Banda returned to the country and was acclaimed as a Messiah. In 1959 there were rumours of a 'murder-plot' to kill all Europeans. A State of Emergency was declared, Dr. Banda and most of the prominent African leaders were arrested, there was widespread rioting and, in the quelling of this, a number of Africans were shot. With the help of Federal troops order was restored: if anything, the opposition to the Federation increased.

A Commission of Inquiry into the events surrounding the Emergency produced a scathing - if often distorted - report, strongly critical of British actions. Mr. Macmillan made a tour of Africa and decided that 'a wind of change' was blowing through the Continent; the time of white rule was over. Dr Banda was released from detention and returned to even greater acclaim.

I narrate the above to describe the situation as it was when I arrived in Nyasaland in May 1960. Coming as we did from West Africa where I had been used to working for African Ministers and with - or sometimes for - African Civil Servants we found racial attitudes in Nyasaland very strange. On the other hand, life was infinitely more comfortable. Food supplies were much better - it was a delight to be able to get fresh pasteurised milk instead of the tinned or powdered variety that we had had to use in Nigeria.

I was posted to the Financial Division, by pure chance since I knew nothing about Government finance or macroeconomics. It was, however, fortunate. My superiors there were men of great ability, although hard taskmasters, and, once I had demonstrated that I could do my work, I was given ever-increasing responsibility. Although a few curious eyes were surreptitiously cast upon my callipered leg, the fact that I was disabled did not matter provided I could do my work as well or better than anyone else.

In late 1962 we were on 'home' leave at Seaview in the Isle of Wight when I received a telephone message from the Colonial Office 'asking' me to attend the Nyasaland Constitutional Conference in London. My job there was little more than that of a dogs-body but I was thrilled to be participating in historic events, however menial my position. I remember returning by train at the weekend, lugging my suitcase onto the ferry then off at the other end carrying it down Ryde pier to the bus that would take me back to my family. I was pretty fit in those days.

On our return to Nyasaland I was given a small 'charge-allowance' in recognition that I was doing a job above my grade. Very shortly after I was detailed to be one of the Ministry of Finance team which was going to London for financial discussions with the U.K. Government. It was all very thrilling, learning something new every day.

From time to time my calliper still gave trouble. The screws holding the struts to the bucket top were of steel, the struts were duralumin that was softer. The screws would work loose and tightening them simply tore holes in their socket. So, while in London, it was always necessary to visit the workshop at Stanmore where Mr. Tuck presided.

Once back in Nyasaland I strained my back so that I was unable to stand upright (or drive a car or go up stairs). Our house was a bungalow (this was the norm for all Government housing) so, as the work couldn't be left, and I couldn't go to it, it had to be brought to me. I don't remember seeing any physiotherapist - indeed I don't think there was one in Zomba - but after about three weeks my back was better. I was advised to sleep on a hard mattress in future (there were no such things in the Public Works Department stores but planks underneath made any mattress hard). I've been very fortunate in that the trouble has never recurred.

On the 1st January 1964 I was appointed a MBE. I was not yet 34.

I stayed in Malawi for seven more years. It was a lovely country, the people as courteous as any in the world. Above all the work was fascinating. The Federation of Rhodesia and Nyasaland ceased to exist on 1 January 1964 and in many fields we were building anew, unfettered by past people and past precedent.

My seniors all left, some feeling too old to adapt to working for an independent African Government, some seeing their opportunity to make a complete change in their pattern of life. I stayed on, was promoted several times in quick succession and eventually headed the Ministry of Finance. These were interesting years, not always easy ones, but never, ever, dull.

This is not the place to write about the economic and financial progress made by Malawi (the new name for the country formerly known as Nyasaland) during this period, astonishing as it was even to me. It was office work, it was business, whether it was negotiating development aid from Western Governments in London, Washington, Copenhagen or Bonn, or ensuring that public monies were properly used. However, the fact that I am disabled played a significant part in some domestic events; these may be of interest to the readers of this memoir.

Monkey Bay is in the southern part of Lake Malawi. It was something of a tourist resort and on one occasion my family and I were lent the use of a cottage there. The water was bilharzia free and we all enjoyed swimming, or at least splashing, around in the shallows. Now it so happened that a young hippopotamus lived in this Bay and swam over to see what we were doing. I am sure that his intentions were pacific but even a young hippopotamus is quite large, has a very big mouth and very big teeth. I had the horrible thought that that mouth and those teeth could do an awful lot of damage to my young children. All I could do though was to put myself between the hippo and them, tell them to get out of the water quickly and quietly, gradually to retreat to the shore myself and just hope that the hippo would lose interest and go away. Fortunately it did.

The event brought home to me, however, how little able I was to protect my family in any physical way.

On another occasion we were driving through Mozambique (then a Portuguese colony). The earth road was deeply rutted by the passing of lorries with a stony ridge running parallel between the ruts. Suddenly I heard a bang, saw the gear change lever jerk into 'Neutral' (I was now the proud owner of a Mercedes-Benz with proper automatic transmission) and the car slowed. When I tried to move the lever to 'Drive' to restore power, nothing happened. The engine was still working but the car gradually slowed to a stop.

After an hour or two we heard the noise of a motorcar and an old VW appeared driven by a Portuguese priest. He stopped, we explained what had happened and he got down on the ground to see what was wrong. But, because of the central ridge I referred to above, there was not enough room for him to crawl underneath. Neither his car jack not mine could be used. Then a lorry came up. That had a big jack and in it were quite a lot of men. My car was lifted up and the priest crawled underneath again. When he re-emerged he said that a rock had hit the transmission system and broken a part. He thought that a temporary repair might be achieved by tying the two broken pieces together. He then told the men to cut tendrils from the surrounding trees and, using these, made the repair. Full of trepidation I re-started the engine and gently, oh so gently, moved the gear-change lever. It worked! With advice not to change gear unless unavoidable (so as to put as little pressure on the joined together pieces), and with a thousand thanks from us to all who had helped, we drove on through the bush for the next hundred miles to our destination.

Once more, though, I was made aware of my inadequacies in the physical field. I could not have crawled under the car, nor jacked it up, nor cut vines. In all matters like this, I depended upon others.

We would fly to England on home leaves, often breaking the journey to visit a country *en route.* On one occasion we stayed in Athens. It was August and searingly hot but my wife and I were keen to see the greatest of the ruins of Greece. The older two of our children were amenable enough but our youngest, aged four and a half, had no interest in 'a lot of stones'! When visiting Mycenae this lack of interest turned into stubborn rebellion. He was determined not to walk up the hill from the car park (to be fair, it was a scorchingly hot day). We couldn't leave him; I could not carry him and my wife felt that she had to be free to help me. Fortunately our eleven-year-old daughter volunteered to carry him; she did and thus we were all able to see the Lion Gate and the tomb of Agamemnon.

On another occasion, visiting Egypt, we drove out to see the Sphinx and the nearby Pyramids (still in desert sand but I believe now almost devoured by the spreading shanty suburbs of Cairo). I would have liked to explore the Pyramids a bit but the narrow and low entry tunnel made this impossible for me. I had to wait outside while the other four were shown the burial chamber where once a Pharaoh had lain.

On the other hand, I <u>was</u> able to climb the steps to the Acropolis of Great Zimbabwe and to marvel at the stone work of that vanished African kingdom.

At my sons' English prep school there was an elderly priest, very gentle, referred to as a saint in a 'Daily Telegraph Magazine' article. On one occasion when I visited the school I talked to him about my family and my life. He asked when I caught polio and when I replied, "In 1955", he reflected a moment and then said, "So Nicholas has never known you as a normal father?" I am sure the comment was not made with any intent to hurt; it was simply a statement of a fact. It was a fact of which I was well aware. The things most fathers do with their sons, playing football with them, going on walks, climbing or sailing, these were things that I could never do. Perhaps I missed this participation more than they did. In any event, there was nothing that could be done about it.

On Government business, as I have said above, I had to make numerous flights to the capitals of 'donor' countries. Although I travelled First Class (Business Class had not yet been introduced), and was appropriately cosseted, these were still very tiring. Airports too were rapidly increasing in size and the walk to or from the airport gate was becoming steadily longer. It never occurred to me to ask for assistance until, one day at Kennedy Airport, an American Airlines ground crew spontaneously offered me a seat in her 'buggy with a fringe on top'. Thereafter I was not too proud to ask!

There were, naturally, still problems from time to time with my calliper. One day, in a meeting in London with the Ministry of Overseas Development, I did nothing more than cross my legs and then heard something snap. A strut had sheared. It was fortunate for me that it had done so in a place where friendly help was immediately at hand. At the end of the meeting I explained what had happened; the Ministry officials phoned the Royal National Orthopaedic Hospital, a Government car was summoned to take me there, the repair was done. Within a few hours I was mobile again.

In 1969 I was appointed a CBE and was notified that I would be invested with this honour at Buckingham Palace. There, I - along with other recipients - was told what to do, when to bow, the position to adopt before the Queen, that after having been invested we should walk backwards before turning to our right to leave the Chamber. All went well with me except, so I was told, that I had failed to take enough steps backwards before turning and had thus partly turned my back on Her Majesty. " I am sure", said the official, "that in your circumstances Her Majesty will be understanding".

I had mentally set myself two targets, that I would end Malawi's current account Budget deficit and that I would hand over my post to a Malawian successor[3]. These I achieved and at the end of 1970 I left the country. My Colonial Service career was over.

---

3. The latter, George Jaffu, with his daughter Fiona, is shown with me in the recent photo at the frontispiece.

England, 1971-73

I travelled back to England by sea with all our baggage and my car, arriving after a slow passage at the end of January, 1971 (my wife had left Malawi earlier than I so as to be with our children during the Christmas holidays).

My first thought was to look for a job. I was under no illusions that finding one would be easy. Admittedly, I had had a successful career to date: but it had been in Africa. My experience there was likely to be regarded as irrelevant to work in Britain. Moreover I was well aware that employers might think twice or thrice before taking on a disabled man of 40.

Job-hunting was made even more difficult by the postal strike that began the day after I landed in England. One could not just post an application in reply to an advertisement; it had to be delivered by hand (this was before the fax revolutionised communications).

After a number of disappointments I was offered a post with the British Steel Corporation, working in London. We were now free to look for a house.

My wife calculated that I should not have to travel more than 40 minutes door-to-door and on this basis, and allowing for my slower-than-average walking pace, decided upon the areas we should focus on. One of these was South Croydon and in August we bought a good-sized Victorian house near that railway-station. It was the first house we had owned in eighteen years of marriage! We intended to make it our home for all our future years.

As a boy I had been interested in - though not particularly skilled at - carpentry. In the cellars of our new house there was ample room to set-up a workshop. An electric saw, sander and polisher, and a number of vices minimised the problems caused by only one useful arm. I enjoyed myself putting up shelves, making window boxes, flooring the attics.

We painted and decorated. Lesley redesigned the garden to make it labour saving and I dug the flowerbeds and put in some new hedges.

I began to learn about steel-making, visited all the major steel-works and admired the ability and sheer hard work of Sir Monty Finniston, then Chief Executive and to be the future Chairman of the Corporation.

In 1972 Britain, which economically had been in boom, began to experience another balance-of-payments crisis. Interest rates (and the cost of a mortgage) went up. Public sector (which included British Steel) salaries were frozen. There were rail strikes and electricity strikes. On one occasion the train on which I was travelling stopped about a quarter of a mile from Victoria Station; passengers had to scramble down from the carriages and walk along the track. Often, at the end of the day, I would find myself at Victoria in a mob of commuters, all waiting for news of a train - any train - that might take them in a homeward direction. At any rumour that a train was in, that a train might be leaving, the mob would rush like lemmings to the platform. I couldn't rush; my fear was that I might fall and be trampled underfoot.

During that winter's electricity strikes our offices were ice-cold. At home the central heating didn't function but, by good fortune, we had kept one open fireplace and there was coal in the cellar. We had kept, also, our oil-lamps from Nigeria; we had light enough.

It was not an easy time for anyone. I found it very difficult.

Moreover, events made me doubt whether our plan to live in England was sensible. There seemed to be no prospect of promotion at work; although salaries were frozen, the cost of living was rising rapidly. However on 1st January 1973 Britain had become a Member State of the European Economic Community. There was an opportunity to get a post in the European Commission (with a very attractive salary). We agonised over which way I should decide. We had both longed for a base in England, a house that our children would be able to think of as 'home'. I felt, also, some personal loyalty to Sir Monty Finniston who had always treated me with kindness. On the other hand, a post in the Commission had all the glamour and excitement of an entirely new beginning and I had always been strongly in favour of strengthening Britain 's links with the countries of Continental Europe. Finally, the financial inducement was almost irresistible. On 1st December 1973 I took up a post in the Directorate-General for Overseas Aid in Brussels.

The European Commission, Brussels, 1973-87
I passed nearly 14 years in Brussels: approaching half of my entire working life. They were begun with hope; they ended with sadness. If, looking back, I was to sum them up in one word, that word would be 'disappointment'.

I was not alone in this. Many 'Brits' of about my age who came to the Commission with the same hopes as I found, like me, that it was difficult to settle. We were almost interlopers into an already established organisation, an organisation, whose working practices were based, quite naturally, on those in the two great founder members, France and Germany. There was nothing wrong with these but they were very different from those to which we were used.

Moreover, although we were supposed to be 'European' first and foremost, we could not dissociate ourselves from what was happening in Britain. For six years we watched Britain decline as an economic power, a decline that it seemed impossible to halt. Then, when Margaret Thatcher became Prime Minister and seemed to halt the decline, she combined this with such an 'anti-European' stance as to alienate most other Member States. I do not know whether I alone felt that this affected me, but feel it I did.

My work involved the giving of Development Aid from the Commission to the former French, Belgian and Dutch colonies, which had now become independent states politically but which were still dependent economically. With Britain's accession, the former British colonies in Africa, the Caribbean and in the Indian and Pacific Oceans were also to benefit from this aid (termed the European Development Fund or EDF it was quite separate from the aid provided direct by Member States).

It involved a lot of travelling and over the years I visited most of the English speaking countries, some several times. When I was the senior member of a group or was travelling by myself I did so as the representative of the Commission and my contacts would always include Ministers of the Country, often its President.

Flights were always long and usually tiring. Inevitably there were occasions when connections were missed and when one would be stuck for hours in an airport, waiting for the next plane. The worst of these occasions was at Calcutta airport trying to get a flight to the then newly- independent country of Bangladesh. The heat and humidity was intense, there was nowhere to wait, and no refreshments were available. Worst of all was the fact that no one knew when a plane would come or if I was booked on it.

On such occasions it was not possible to tell Commission staff at one's destination what had happened. Plans for meetings, hotel bookings, arrangements for travel within the destination country, all these had to be discarded, only to be set up anew when at last one arrived.

Once, when flying to Guyana, I found myself stranded at Port-of-Spain in Trinidad. While waiting here, tired after a flight which had already lasted, with delays, about 16 hours, I tripped on a 'sleeping policeman' and grazed my knee quite badly. It was a hot day, no planes were due for some hours, the airport was asleep and no medical staff were around. The only thing I had available to sterilise the graze was 'After-Shave'. It stung but the graze did not turn septic.

My entire life and work in Brussels, however, was over- shadowed by the sudden death of my wife. This calamity took place about two years after I had moved to Brussels.

She had been my inspiration, my comforter and my support throughout our marriage and, particularly, since I had caught polio. The thought that she might be the first to die had never crossed my mind. The rapid onset of the leukaemia that caused her death gave no period for adjustment. Time heals many wounds but this is one that has remained unhealed.

My daughter was herself married and living in England. Both my sons were with me in Brussels. I could give them a roof over their heads and food to eat but I could not create a home for them. In any event over the next few years they would themselves be due to move on.

There followed other deaths, of my father and of my mother, of Lesley's mother (her father had died while we were in Malawi) and of my mother's sister (who had played an important part in my own upbringing when my parents were in Malaya and I was at school in England). My brother, who was very close to me, was working in Hong Kong: the other side of the world.

The year before Lesley died I had been thrown off-balance while on an escalator which took me down to my office car-park space. This was not moving when I got on it and I assumed that it was out of order. Then it started, catching me wrong footed. The tread under my left leg, rigid in its calliper, rose and as it did so I was thrust forward and down, my head landing on the gratings at the base of the escalator. I could easily have been killed. As it was, my left arm, my only working arm, was very badly broken. It was to be almost four months before I was able to return to work.

During these months Lesley had had to care for me almost as if I was a baby; I was able to do little more than an infant could.

Although the bone mended around the steel pin, I do not think that I have ever regained full use of the arm.

Two years after her death I developed kidney stones. An operation was necessary to cut them out.

The next year I caught pleurisy. I had had pneumonia while in Malawi and quite bad bronchitis during my first year in Brussels; on both occasions my limited lung capacity greatly exacerbated the effects of the illness. On this occasion my lungs almost filled with fluid which had to be drained off. However, the heartsack was also affected and a separate puncture had to be made to prevent the heart from being drowned. I had been given a local anaesthetic only and it was quite frightening lying there, watching the surgeon decide upon exactly where to insert the needle. This unease was not lessened by my knowledge that earlier in the day he had had great difficulty in locating and hitting one of my veins!

One incident had its amusing side - at least to an onlooker. One winter morning I opened the front door to see if there was snow on the path leading to my car. Everything looked to be clear but no sooner had I shut the front door behind me and taken a step forward than my legs shot from under me and down I went; the path was coated in black ice. I couldn't get up; here was nothing that I could do but lie there - getting steadily colder - and hope that someone would notice my predicament. The first few passers-by paid no attention. I began to worry. Then a small girl past, presumably on her way to school. I called out. Rather doubtfully she approached. I tried explaining what had happened but she was clearly a bit suspicious. Eventually though she agreed to *"Sonnez à la porte"* (ring the door-bell). This brought my younger son, Julian, down from his bed. He opened the door, the little girl scuttled away, and he was able to pull me into the house where I was stood up and thawed out. I was never able to thank the unknown little girl.

I did not escape so lightly from my next fall. One night when going from bed to the bathroom, without my calliper as I had been in bed, but holding my left leg straight as I had been taught to do at Osborne fifteen years before, I lost my balance. I fell with my whole weight on my left knee, the shock being carried up through my femur. The head of the bone splintered. I was alone in my flat and it was not until the next day that help became available. It was a very painful night.

At the hospital an operation was performed to insert a pin in the femur and to cap the head of the splintered bone. The operation was a success but it was some months before it was thought that the newly knit bone could bear my weight, even with the calliper struts taking most of it. Psychologically also the accident left its mark. I never again had the confidence to walk without my calliper and, even with it, I was wary lest I fall (which I was still to do very often: but less calamitously than on this occasion).

From then on I have used a typist's stool on castors (but with the back removed) to get from my bed to the bathroom before dressing and putting on my calliper and again at night before going to bed. It takes up much less space than any normal wheelchair.

In 1981 I re-married, to an extremely nice and kind young Belgian. Sadly, and through no fault of hers, the marriage did not last and in 1986 we separated. Happily we have remained very good friends; she re-married and has a daughter and we keep in regular touch through telephone calls and letters. She and her family have visited me in England and I meet them when I go to Belgium. This I count great good fortune.

The ending of my marriage caused me, however, to re-examine my position. I was doing no more than camping - as it were - in Brussels. I was not at home there. I had made few close friends; my children were all living in England. There was an opportunity to take early retirement. My daughter urged that I take it on the grounds that sooner or later I would return to England and that it was better to do so when still young enough to adapt to an almost foreign country.

I took her advice and in mid 1987 retired from the European Commission. My paid working life was at an end.

Author, 1954

Early Steps, August 1955

*Author, 1956, in Enugu, E. Nigeria, with daughter,
Caroline, aged two years.*

With daughter, Caroline, Abak, Eastern Nigeria, 1959

Nung Ibesit Leper Village, Abak, Eastern Nigeria, 1959

With Caroline and Julian at The Acropolis, Athens, 1965

SUCOMA Sugar Mill, Malawi, 1968
(from left) unknown, Author; John Tembo (Minister of Finance), Gerald Percy (General Manager; LONRHO Malawi)

With Douglas Williams, Under-Secretary, UK Overseas Development Administration and George Jaffu, Under-Secretary, Malawi Treasury. IMF/IBRD Governor's Meeting, Washington, 1968.

Retirement 1987 - Now

I viewed the prospect of living in England as a retired person with some concern. Naturally, I had visited England many times since I had taken up my Colonial Service career in 1954 - I had even lived in England for almost three years (1971-73). Nevertheless, although not at all a 'foreign' land, I did not feel quite at home with either the country or its people. My memories were of a country that had changed.

I was older now, also, and in many ways less able to adapt or to cope with new problems than when last I had actually lived in England. Then, too, I had had a wife who managed the domestic side of our life, things that I would now have to do. I was worried also about money, quite needlessly. My pension was much less than the salary I had been receiving, of course, but it was to prove amply sufficient to live comfortably.

Soon after my arrival in England, and while I was still casting about, a friend put me in touch with a local 'Access Group'. Until this occasion, I had had no contact with any disabled people (except my daughter's godmother, Elizabeth Twistington Higgins) since I had left Stanmore in 1955. Indeed, since then my approach to life had been that I was not disabled: ridiculous though that may sound. The business of living, the need to convince others that I could do almost anything that able-bodied persons could do had taken all my time and energy. Now, however, English society was changing; the existence of a 'disability' was no longer something which had to be kept out of sight as if it were shameful. My own position too had changed. I no longer had to prove myself in a career. I had time to meet other disabled people, to learn from their experiences, to benefit from the changes they had wrought while I was abroad, time, also, in which I might be able to assist others.

First, though, I had to find somewhere to live. After much searching and some false starts, I settled on a new 'sheltered housing' development in Hungerford. Hungerford was an ideally sized town for me, large enough to provide all necessary local services, not too large to swamp me. 'Sheltered housing' meant that assistance was always available in an emergency but that I could still live an independent life. Hungerford had good road communications as well; I could visit my children who were all in the London area at the time, my brother whose home was in Surrey, my only surviving cousin living in Winchester.

I felt the need for someone who could manage the domestic side of my life, the cooking and cleaning, the buying of provisions, the care of my clothes. I was most fortunate in that a lady, living in a nearby village, was anxious to augment her income (her husband had become redundant at the same time I was looking for somewhere to live). Her upbringing, education and experience indicated that she would be an ideal choice. So it has proved. Without her I would not have been able to live the life that I have done during the past eleven years.

The furnishing of my ground-floor flat, the discarding of furniture that was too large or otherwise unsuitable, the purchase of curtains, carpets, kitchen utensils and some new furniture to replace the old, all these things took up much time. My new flat was suitable in general but a bath was potentially dangerous; it had to be removed and replaced with a shower containing a seat to which I could transfer safely. The floor of the little conservatory opening off the sitting room was a few inches lower than in the sitting room itself, of no consequence to a fully mobile person but a possible hazard to me.

I discovered to my surprise and delight how many items were on the market to help people with disabilities. Newsletters published by the different disability groups, catalogues by commercial firms, displays at the Disabled Living Foundation, all these appeared to cater with abundant choice for any imaginable impairment: all that was needed was the money to buy them.

I found Velcro a tremendous boon; it might not hold a collar together quite as smartly as a button but it was infinitely easier to fasten than doing up a button one-handed. It was of equal help replacing the cuff buttons on the left sleeve of my shirt. More recently I have used a Velcro buckle to secure my shoe instead of a lace.

A daughter-in-law had introduced me to the microwave. This and the enormous range of chilled and frozen meals now available in super-markets meant that feeding oneself should present no problem - providing that one could undo the packaging, of course.

The car had been - still is - my principal mobility aid. Automatic transmission as a factory built-in feature had become available, I was glad to note, on ever-smaller cars. Power steering, too, was no longer confined to the larger models. During a visit to a 'Mobility Road-Show' at Crowthorne my younger son noticed a 'Magic-Ball' manufactured by Brian Page which let one use all the most essential instruments without taking a hand off the steering wheel. This has much increased my safety as a driver. Since then I have become aware of a host of other modern driving-aids helpful to all motorists not only those who are disabled, e.g. an infrared sensor, which when the motorist is backing, warns of the approach to an obstacle.

During the time that I was making all these fascinating discoveries I was also pursuing contacts with other disabled people and the information and action groups that they had set up. I got in touch with - and became a member of - the British Polio Fellowship (I have been astounded over the years to see how many 'old polios' had distinguished themselves - and to be grateful for their friendship). A new 'Disabled Club' was being formed in Hungerford and I was asked to become its Treasurer; this began the widening of my acquaintance in the town. I learned that the District Council had set up a 'Liaison Group on Disability' and I began attending its meetings. I had a great deal to learn but, with helpful mentors, I was making a beginning.

Over the succeeding years I have held various positions in this latter Group, helping in the production of three fully revised editions of an 'Access Guide' as well playing a part in ensuring that the needs of people with disabilities were kept in mind by the local community as a whole. Berkshire was one of the earliest counties selected by the Government to create a Disability Information service and BDIN (as the Berkshire service came to be called) proved to be highly effective. The Newbury Citizens Advice Bureau under an outstanding manager played a major local role in this and for some years I was a member of its Management Committee.

At a national level, I was invited by the Director of the Royal Association for Disability and Rehabilitation (RADAR) - himself an 'old polio' from childhood - to sit on their International Committee. Later, I represented RADAR on the committee of HELIOS and of the latter's successor organisation, the UK Disability Forum for Europe. This Forum, along with similar bodies in other Member States of the European Union, ensures that the needs of people with disabilities all over Europe are brought to the attention of the European Commission and Parliament. I also had the good fortune to work with John Groom's and to see how that charity, while retaining the Christian values of its founder, was searching out ways in which it could meet the needs of our present age.

During these ten years I have met with many disabled men and women who have overcome their own disabilities, physical, aural, visual. Their courage, determination and cheerfulness have filled me with admiration. Through their efforts over the past forty years people with disabilities have emerged from behind the curtain where they had been kept even if they are not yet full 'equal citizens'. However, the help given by 'able-bodied' people (I loathe these phrases but there seems no way of avoiding their use!) should not be forgotten or begrudged. Sometimes it may be clumsy physically, giving pain as much as help; sometimes, it may be offered insensitively through ignorance rather than intent. Where it is clearly well-meaning, however, I try to accept it in the spirit in which it is offered and with a cheery smile - even if my teeth are gritted (invisibly I hope!).

Similarly, although voluntary organisations of and controlled by disabled people should clearly be the desirable norm, there should be welcome room for those who fall outside these criteria - the 'non-disabled' should be seen as allies rather than as a threat to our independence. After all, there are more of them!

I must, however, leave preaching and return to my own tale.

I have written above of my involvement with disability organisations. Other interests also have occupied my time, membership of Ant-Slavery International being prominent among these. Visits to London, sometimes on business, often on pleasure, and holidays in Europe have featured regularly.

On these, accidents have continued to happen. On one occasion in Brussels my calliper strut fractured for no apparent reason. I had no spare with me - sheer lack of thought as I had had ample room in my car. My helper had to fly over bringing a replacement while I remained helpless in a hotel room. On another occasion in London I slipped in the shower and fractured my right elbow; the drive back to Hungerford was quite painful. On a third, coming out of a hotel in Kensington, I had a spectacular fall. I overlooked the small lintel on the front door, tripped and fell forward and down, over the flight of 6 or 7 steps, landing on the pavement to the astonishment of the taxi-driver who was awaiting me. 'Born to be hanged', I was shaken but unhurt.

I am conscious of the fact that references to 'falls' appear rather often in this narrative (although there have been many more by far than those mentioned). They have affected me physically when bones have been broken; even when they have not, the emotional effect of being temporarily helpless, of having to wait - sometimes for some unknowable period of time - for this to be obtained, must not be lost sight of. One is conscious that every step may bring one down.

Indeed, almost every action brings home - consciously or unconsciously - the fact of one's disability. It may be on a very small scale; for instance the difficulty of trying to insert papers into a plastic sleeve. It may be frustration at the sheer waste of so much precious time waiting for others because one does not wish to try their patience by making them wait for you. It is always with you, however well disguised.

Over the next half-century I think that miniature power-aids, biology and medicine should compensate for many physical defects. Many diseases, also, may be eradicated. For example, Polio, the disease that has caused my most obvious physical disabilities, has existed from the early days of mankind's existence. In the 'developed' world, thanks to Salk and Sabin, it is now almost unknown and young doctors say that they have never seen a case, never even seen a person paralysed as a result of it. The World Health Organisation even predicts that it is possible to envisage the eradication of the virus within five years. I pray that this may be so. The almost incredible news that two million children in Sri Lanka were vaccinated on one day in early October demonstrates what can be done: an achievement enhanced in that it was carried out against the background of many years of violent inter-racial strife.

For many years yet, however, there will be a need to look after the dwindling number of survivors whose health and physical condition can only deteriorate.

I think that it was about twenty years ago when 'old polios' began to note that their physical strength was declining, that they had more fatigue, greater breathlessness after any exertion and pain. Some thought that live polio virus, which had remained dormant since the original attack and was now re-appearing, caused these effects, termed Post Polio Syndrome (PPS). Others, sceptical, asserted that the symptoms were no more than could be expected from old age.

There was bitter debate, particularly in the United States but also in Britain on this matter about the time I returned to England. A great number of research studies were conducted (the contents fill many volumes) and it appeared that the symptoms related more to the number of years that had passed since polio was contracted[4] than to the physical age of the sufferer. In other words, it is more than just 'old age' which is responsible.

The most common theory at present is that after a polio infection some of the surviving motor neurones "sprout" and

---

4. Typically, 30 to 40 years.

may take on responsibility for from five to ten times as many muscle fibres as before. The more the individual then does for the rest of his life, the greater the likelihood that these post-polio muscles may deteriorate. Sometimes, this deterioration may be sudden - as Sir Julian Critchley describes in his Foreword happened to him - sometimes it may become apparent more slowly: individual susceptibility may vary.

Whether I am suffering from this Late Effects of Polio (LEP), I do not know. Certainly there is the increased breathlessness, a greater lack of strength when doing things and increased fatigue afterwards (and an increased tendency to fall) which have been noted as symptoms of it. But these symptoms could have other causes too, such as age or overweight (which I too evidently am!). Fortunately, whether for LEP or for simple ageing, the action to be taken is much the same. Physical inactivity is to be avoided; it will lead to further weakness and may increase the risk of other degenerative diseases. On the other hand, overstraining one's remaining muscles may lead to them breaking down. So a mean must be struck - although this is more easily written than done!

I have written above about using a 'buggy' or a wheelchair at airports. This did not worry me. Similarly, I had no difficulties about using them at railway stations (particularly as I needed help getting into or out of most carriages). For a long time, however, I resisted using a wheelchair on other occasions: to do so I felt was a surrender. Here too, though, the passing years and reduced muscular strength (and, I fear, increased weight!) have forced me into recognising that if I want to do some things, to visit some places, then I must also accept the use of a wheelchair. I did so with rather ill grace and indeed many of my fears about it were confirmed. As other people with disabilities have found, once in a wheelchair pushed by a carer or friend one is regarded as an inanimate object by most of the public. It is not made easier by the fact that one's 'pusher' can't easily hear what you are saying (or vice-versa)!

It is, of course, only one's pride that suffers.

Happily, my impression is that the general public is becoming increasingly 'disability aware' and more conscious of the need - and the common politeness - of addressing the 'pushed' as well as the 'pusher'. Furthermore, new technology has resulted in the much greater availability of compact and self-controlled powered chairs. Lifts can be fitted into many cars of the station-wagon or people carrier type and, at the touch of a button, these can lift the wheelchair from the car, lower it to the road or pavement ready for use and, when the task is done, lift the chair back into the car. All this without physical exertion. Mobility with the retention of personal independence is at hand.

However, technical aids such as these (and also all the other equipment I have referred to earlier) have to be paid for. The State Benefits. Attendance Allowance, Mobility Allowance, etc., - while welcome - meet only a fraction of the costs that face a 'person with disabilities' trying to lead a 'normal life'. Hidden or unhidden, society does not have, perhaps does not wish to have, any knowledge of quite how large these costs are.

About fifteen years ago the Ministry of Overseas Development (as then it was) supported an application that I should receive some compensation for the disabilities caused by the polio caught while a serving officer. They did all they could and thought that they had surmounted every obstacle. Then came the UK Treasury. This body ruled that, while in principle I met all the criteria, compensation was payable only to reflect loss of earning power. 'Since Mr. Barnes has had a successful subsequent career, no such loss is apparent'! It was a neat, skillful and unplayable response by the guardians of the public purse which, as a civil servant, I could not but admire. 'Game, set and match' to them.

You must understand that I know that I have been, and am, much more fortunate than are the great majority of other disabled people, whatever their form of impairment. My life is 'financially-comfortable'; really, I lack for nothing. Above all, as I hope I've made clear in this memoir, I have found, and still do, that life is crammed with interest; the past 43 years have been fuller by far than could be expected. I have rejoiced in the love of my family and the companionship of friends. I am grateful for what I have had; I look forward with interest to what is to come; with God's will, I hope that I may continue to play my part.